Holy Spirit at Work
Children's Version

Dr. Carolyn D. Cecil, D.Min.
Illustrated by Janet Utley Wimmer

Holy Spirit at Work

Children's Version

An introduction to Lord Holy Spirit
for Children

Dr. Carolyn D. Cecil, D.Min.
Illustrated by Janet Utley Wimmer

ARPress

ARPress
45 Dan Road Suite 5
Canton MA 02021

Hotline: 1(888) 821-0229
Fax: 1(508) 545-7580

Ordering Information:
Quantity sales. Special discounts are available on quantity purchases by corporations, associations, and others. For details, contact the publisher at the address above.

Printed in the United States of America.
ISBN-13:   Paperback   979-8-89676-303-1
                eBook   979-8-89676-304-8

Library of Congress Control Number: 2024925147

Holy Spirit at Work

Children's Version

Our Earth is big and round,
With blue oceans and green ground.
God chose this planet for us all,
Because it is not too big and not too small!

Father God is on the Throne,
His Son at His right hand.
Lord Holy Spirit is everywhere,
On the water and on the land.

Holy Spirit is doing the work down here,
Earth is His job site.
He is getting people saved as fast as He can,
On the left and on the right.

The day people say "yes" to Jesus,
They get the Holy Spirit too.
He stays with believers forever,
Living right inside of you.

Holy Spirit is God,
He is one in three.
God the Father, God the Son,
God the Spirit, now you see.

Our God is a good God,
There is nothing He cannot do.
He is sending angels and the Holy Spirit
To watch closely over you!

For God so
loved the
world...

that He gave
His only Son
John 3:16

Like the wind, the Holy Spirit
Cannot ever be seen,
But His effects are everywhere,
North to south and in between.

Lord Holy Spirit never goes to bed,
And never takes a nap.
He goes everywhere on Earth,
And He does not need a map!

Some do not know He is here,
Often He is ignored.
He just wants to be welcomed,
Loved, and adored.

Holy Spirit is right all the time,
He is never wrong!
Listen carefully to His words,
And let Him lead you along.

Holy Spirit is your helper and guide;
He will always be at your side!
He is your comforter and friend,
In Him you can confide!

He rides with you in cars and trucks;
He really likes the train.
He is right beside you on long trips,
Or in the jet airplane.

Lord Holy Spirit is so kind;
He is gentle as a dove.
Everything He ever does,
Is done out of His love!

Lord Holy Spirit is just like us,
In several important ways.
He has thoughts, emotions, and feelings,
And loves us all our days.

Unconditional love is
The Spirit's most important theme.
Teaching us to love like Him,
Is His greatest dream.

Holy Spirit sees all as precious;
He calls each one a treasure.
Be tender toward His people,
That will give Him pleasure!

Always pay attention to Him,
He knows just what to do!
He has a still small voice,
A whisper to guide you.

Sometimes it is hard to hear Him,
He is quiet as a mouse!
The best time to pray is when
It is quiet in the house.

12

The Bible tells us that Jesus,
Had the Holy Spirit too.
The Holy Spirit gave Him power,
And now the Holy Spirit lives in you.

Jesus and the Holy Spirit,
Did miracles every day.
He worked with all the people,
And helped them in every way.

Jesus went all around,
Healing sickness and disease.
The Holy Spirit did the work,
Because that is His expertise.

14

The Holy Spirit is good at healing
And setting people free.
He can heal a broken heart,
Because that is His specialty.

He knows just what to do
To cause the pain to ease.
He calms emotions too,
When people get on their knees!

When you get sick or troubled,
Ask friends to come and pray.
The Holy Spirit will come to visit
And take the hurts away.

Holy Spirit helps the pastors preach,
He helps the teachers teach.
The Holy Spirit can help you every day,
And help you grow in any way.

Holy Spirit helps members to
Witness, evangelize, and pray.
He visits all the church buildings,
And camp sites every day!

He is full of signs and wonders,
He gives visions and dreams.
He does a billion jobs at once,
At least that is how it seems!

Holy Spirit goes to school,
He goes to every class.
He helps the teacher teach,
He helps the students pass!

When you grow up
And decide what you want to do,
The Lord Holy Spirit
Will always be with you!

With the Holy Spirit,
You can plan great things to do.
He will come along,
And make your dreams come true.

An argument with a teacher,
Family, friends, or Mom,
Does not happen naturally,
It comes from the Bad one!

The Holy Spirit can be hurt,
When you choose to do bad.
He only wants the best for you,
And meanness makes Him sad.

The Holy Spirit helps you
To make better choices.
Problems always come from
Listening to the wrong voices.

When people get in fights,
Or things do not go right,
The Holy Spirit is in your heart,
And Jesus will give you a brand new start.

If you are really scared,
You can talk to Him anytime.
He will be there when you call on Him,
No need to wait in line.

All problems must be given to Him,
He can work them out.
Forgive others and forgive yourself,
That is what it is all about!

Father God has a big, big, house,
And He wants everyone to fill it.
He has a big, big book,
And He wants your name written in it!

God wants all the people,
In every village, town, and nation.
He is not satisfied with half the people,
He wants the whole creation!

The whole world filled with the Spirit
Is His idea of fun.
The Holy Spirit will not give up,
Until the work is done!

He is busy, oh so busy,
His work is never done!
But being there to help you
Is His idea of fun!

When Lord Holy Spirit gives His Word,
That is what He will do.
There are no mights, ifs, or maybes,
Because His words are true!

The Precious Holy Spirit
Is just a prayer away.
While this story is at the end,
The Holy Spirit will always stay!

28

A Children's Introduction to Lord Holy Spirit:
This book was written because
Lord Holy Spirit is your friend.
Don't miss out on this relationship,
Just because you cannot see Him!

Other Books by Carolyn Cecil:

Holy Spirit at Work
Life on Earth, What a Journey
Our Good Earth
Simple Holiday Pleasures
Smells to Treasure
Angels at Work
Angels at Work: Elementary Version
Equipped: Equipping and Empowerment for
Christians and Lay Ministers Vol. 1, 2, 3